Digital engineer, Traditional engineer

Ernst van Baar

Digital engineer, Traditional engineer

Ernst van Baar

DEDICATION

Coming together is a beginning. Keeping together is progress. Working together is success.
Henry Ford – 1863-1947 - Founder of the Ford Motor Company

For Niels, Lars, Matthea and for people who make digital engineering great.
And for all the amazing people that make our lives better.

To avoid criticism, say nothing, do nothing, be nothing.

- ARISTOTLE -

CONTENTS

Digital engineer, Traditional engineer – 1

Chapter one – 4

    Lesson one

Chapter two – 8

    Saturday lessons

Chapter three – 31

    Transformation

Chapter four – 44

    Becoming digital

Acknowledgments – 72

Index – 73

About the author – 76

Notes – 77

Digital engineer, Traditional enginee

When I was 23 years old, I had two friends, a digital focuse engineer, and a traditional engineer. One was highly educate and intelligent. He went in the Netherlands to the Del university to do his advanced engineering studies. The digi focused friend only finished secondary school.

Both friends are working hard in their lives. Both a earning good incomes. Yet, one always struggled in his care The other would become one of the most successful engine I know. Both men are great engineers and offered me advi but they did not advice the same things. Both friends believ strongly in education but did not recommend the same stu

If I had only one friend, I would have had to accept reject his advice. Having two friends offered me the choice contrasting points of views. One who is a digital focu engineer and one who is a traditional engineer.

Instead of simply accepting or rejecting one or the oth found myself thinking more comparing and then choosing myself, the problem was that the digital focused engineer not successful yet and the traditional engineer was not successful.

For example, one friend would say. "The love technology is the root for all evil and will replace our jobs.

The other said" If computers can do our job, the computers will do our job." Having two strong friends both influencing me was difficult. I wanted to be a good friend and listen, but the two friends did not say the same things. The contrast in their points of view particularly about developing engineering products was so extreme that I grew curious and intrigued. I began to start thinking for a long period of time about what each was saying.

Because I had two great engineering as friends. I learned from both of them. I had to think about each friend's advice and in doing so I gained valuable insight into the power and effect of one's thoughts on one's life. For example, one friend had a habit of saying. "I need to serve the client." the other friend insisted me to ask. "How can I serve the client better?" One is a statement and the other is a question one lets you off the hook and the other forces you to think. Although both friends are working hard, I noticed that one friend had a habit of putting his brain to sleep when it came to developing engineering products and the other had the habit of exercising his brain. Proper physical exercise increases your chances for health and proper mental exercise increases your chances for wealth. One friend recommended to ask the question. " What does the client want us to become?" The other friend recommended to ask the question. "What do we want our client to become?"

One said, "How can we be the cheapest and win more projects?" the other said. "Don't play the race to the bottom, but how can we do better projects for better clients?"

The power of our thoughts may never be measured or appreciated but it became more obvious to me as a young engineer that it was more important to be aware of my thoughts and how I expressed myself. I noticed that my traditional friend was not really successful not because of the amount of money he earned which was significant but because of his thoughts and actions. As a young engineer having two friends, I became aware of being careful about which thoughts I chose to adopt as my own. Should I listen to my digital focused successful engineering friend or my traditional engineering friend? I was more intrigued by my digital focused friend, so I decided to learn from him.

Chapter one: Lesson one

I met my friend that Saturday morning at 9:00 o'clock and he was already busy, I think being at work for more than one hour. Once he was finished, he pulled up a chair to sit down with me and he asked. "Are you ready?" I nodded my head as I pulled my chair away from the wall to sit in front of him, he was a big man about 1.92 meter and 190 pounds. "Okay, here's my offer." he said. " I will teach you, but I won't do it classroom style. You work from me; I will teach you. You don't work for me; I won't teach you. I can teach you faster if you work, and I'm wasting my time if you just want to sit and listen like you do in school. That's my offer, take it or leave it."

With a teasing smile. "I take it". I said. So, he continued, " I will pay you two euro's an hour and you will work six hours every Saturday." " But I have a football match on each Saturday." I said to my friend. "Take it or leave it." he said. "I will take it" I replied. Choosing to work and learn instead of playing football on Saturday.

For five weeks I worked six hours a day. Creating mainly 2D drawings in a CAD application and around 2:00 PM when my work was done, I went to my friend's assistant, and she dropped me twelve euros in my hand. Now even at the age of 23, twelve euros wasn't really exciting. One beer was around two euros already. The next Saturday I was ready to quit. I had agreed to work only because I wanted to learn and to how to be a successful engineer and to learn from my friend. And now

I was a slave for two euros per hour and on top of that I have not spoken to my friend since that first Saturday. So, I went to my friend and told him I'm going to quit. This time my friend smiled. "Why are you laughing?" I asked him with anger and frustration." I understand you want to have a raise or are you going to quit." my friend says. You said that you would teach me if I worked for you. Well, I have worked for you, I've worked hard creating a lot of drawings. Giving up my football game on Saturday to work for you but you haven't kept your word and you haven't taught me anything. The only thing he said, "not bad". In less than six weeks you sound like most of the students. Not understanding what he was saying.

I continued with my grievance I thought you were going to keep your rent at the bargain and teach me instead you want to torture me. And that's cruel. "I'm teaching you." my friend said. "What have you taught me, nothing." I said angry. " You haven't even talked to me once I agreed to work for two euros per hour." "Wow" my friend said, " now you sound just like my most students. But you're the first person who have ever asked me to teach them how to be successful in engineering I met a lot of students but not one of them asked me what to know about success. They asked me for a job and a paycheck but never to teach me how to be successful so most will spend the best years of their lives working for money. Asked what they have been told but not really understanding what it is they are working for." I sat there listening intensely. "So, what is the lesson I learned from working for you only for two euros per hour." I asked. "That you are cheap. Keep that attitude and you will learn nothing. "What should I do" I asked, "just to take these two euros per hour and smile?" So, my friend smiled and continued "That's the way what the others will do. That's all they do. Working harder, doing more with less, it's a race to the bottom."

I sat staring at the floor beginning to understand the lesson my friend was presenting I could sense it. It was a taste of life, finally. I looked up and asked. "So, what will solve the problem?" "This" he said leaning forward in his chair, the stuff between your ears. It was the moment that I had this magical moment where I realized that this is the lesson which I called lesson number one. Traditional engineers are working for their engineering products. The digital engineers, the engineering products are working for them.

On that Saturday morning I learned a completely different point of view from what I have been taught at my university at the age of 23. I understood that both friends wanted me to learn. Both friends encouraged me to study but not the same thing. My highly educated friend recommended me what he did, study hard get good grades so you can find a safe and secure job with a big company. My digital focused friend wanted me to learn how to be successful and how engineering products can work for me.

"Learning to be successful and let the engineering product work for you is a completely different course of study." I asked "absolutely" my friend answered me "absolutely". We sat in silence on that beautiful Saturday morning. Ready to learn?" asked my friend. "Absolutely!" I said.

I decided to use my Saturdays from now on to study and ask better questions. What is the right size projects, what are digital engineering products? What does technology want from us? What do people want? So many questions crossed in that moment my mind and I realized a lot of new things am I going to learn, and I can't wait!

Chapter two – Saturday lessons

I'm a fan of aviation and that was the first topic I started with. Knowing that after spending more than 25 billion dollars and shipping just a couple of hundred planes, Airbus cancelled the A380 project. During that same period of time, planes that seated 150-200 people did do great. They sold at record numbers they were flown around the world so what's going on here? We have to be really clear about what the appropriate size of a project is because perhaps we have been persuaded that our job is to change the world with a very grand gesture. Maybe we don't want to change the world, my traditional engineering friend say: "I'd rather just do my job" and my digital focused friend say: "how to change the world in a really big and dramatic ways."   But here's the truth: everyone changes the world every single day, not the whole world but part of the world. If you burn any carbon, you're changing the world, if you have kids, you change the world, if you don't have kids, you are changing the world. You change the world when you give somebody a smile or let them in front of you in the line and you change the world when you cut them off.

We change the world when we launch a mid-size project. We change the world when we cancel our project. If you're going to change the world you might as well change it in the way that you can be proud of, so we begin with this idea of resilience.

All of us get to do projects. I realized that a career is a series of projects, a project might be a job where you are doing the same thing every day for a long time, a project might be a book like this. But we pick projects, we pick projects, we work on projects, and we ship projects and having good judgement about which projects to pick is critically important.

If you pick the right project and allocate the right resources to it. It will be more likely to accomplish your goal. Because the opportunity cost of what we choose to do is enormous. In case of Airbus, for that same amount of money during the same period of time what could have been developed   instead?

What does something make the right size project? It depends on who we are seeking to change and who we are seeking to reach. If you are trying to raise money for your non-profit. Identifying five people who can each give you a sizable donation and overwhelming those people with the goodness, with the fit, with the respect, with the dignity, with the preparation that you do. It's going to be way more likely that they donate. Instead, if you identify five thousand people from some list and spin the wheel and hope for the best.

What it means to have a project is that you are predicting the future. We are predicting not only that a project will work that will resonate for the people we seek to serve and to change but the world will be the same when the project is finished.

The longer it takes to bring your project to the world the more likely it is that a someone beat us to it, the more likely it is that by the time the product is done the world doesn't need the product or the project the way we thought it did. And so, when the world changes what would you do? In the case of the Airbus 380 project, they thought they were being super resilient. They built one version for fancy first-class flyers, one version or hope to build one version for people who are going to ship freight like DHL and FedEx. They thought they had it all figured out.

Unfortunately, when you discover that the Airlines around the world are not going to lineup for your very specific elephant. It becomes a white elephant. It turns out that you can't adjust easily because the design wasn't particularly resilient. That as market demands changed, it was too hard to change what they were building.

Journey of the new way, not traditional

If an engineer who thinks that a strong bridge can build from Lego, the engineer will build a bridge that will probably hurt someone. Engineering is about proof. If you can build a strong bridge out of Lego. Show me. If your bridge is better than my bridge, I will accept it. That's totally different then saying, prove me wrong because I believe I'm right. What we seek in engineering is someone who eagerly wants to be proven wrong, because if we are proven wrong it means that we found something better.

Better is a pretty useless term, for the most things we use, design, or buy, the answer is complicated. The drawings which we are used to in the construction process might be a good and proven way of communicating so we can build a strong bridge. If there is a new way of designing and communicating where there are no drawings used, but it's increasing the certainty of making sure that the bridge is going to fit in and is not clashing with the surroundings. What test would need to be done for you to change your mind and proof that is a better way? If you are an engineer and you are building a road or bridge, and you are doing your job properly. It's the journey of exploring new ways and what you are doing is eagerly looking for something to proof you wrong. Because changing your mind is proof that you are doing something right.

Happy with boring

It's tempting to make a boring product or service for everyone in our engineering world. Boring, because boring is beyond criticism. It meets spec and causes no tension because it's for everyone, because if everyone is happy then no one is unhappy. The problem is happy people seems to be happy with boring. It might be a good product or service and it meets spec. But a great product, great idea or service tells a story. It's changing not everyone, but someone. New and boring don't easily go together. The people who are happy with boring aren't looking for a way to make it better. Let's imagine, in two weeks' time a company shows up with services and products which meet spec. They are local with solid products and services, but boring. Are you going to join? Are you happy with boring or are you going to make a difference and making a change happen in our engineering industry?

The other way to read this: prove yourself wrong with the new ideas you have. Well, you are not always wrong, sometimes you will be right. But most of the time, you will be wrong and that's okay.

Race to the top not the bottom

Let's start with a great quote from co-founder Apple Steve Wozniak:" True innovation is one that improves people's lives". But what does this mean? It's no surprise that most companies are relying on selling products and services for their growth and profitability. But product-as-a-service is fundamentally a different business model, so let's have a closer look how this resonates with the quote from Steve Wozniak.

The focus in this model is on the outcomes for the people you seek to serve, not on the input or the product that the company manufactures. Why is this important? Let's look at Rolls-Royce, which sells jet engines to its airline customers. In the traditional service model, every engine problem and maintenance need were a revenue opportunity for Rolls-Royce, the incentive for Rolls-Royce and its airline customers were not aligned. However, under the outcome-based model, Roll-Royce is paid only for every hour the plane is flying, thus aligning the incentives for both parties.

Moving Upstream

Get stuck on a cycle of response, put out fires, dealing with emergencies. Handling one problem after another and perhaps we never get around to fix the system that caused the problem.

That's one reason why we tend to favor reaction: Because it's more tangible, you can call it Downstream and is easier to see and easier to measure but it's a finite game. The opposite of Downstream is Upstream. These are the efforts intended to prevent problems before they happen. Upstream is a similar word for preventing or proactive but the word upstream is the infinite game of pushing further into the direction and not as specific destination. Teaching kids to swim is an excellent upstream way to prevent drownings.

Few years ago, we flipped to "upstream" hot water maintenance. We had this problem with hot water and heating, so we called a company. When he visited, he offered a subscription model. The idea that they'd visit on regular basis – not requiring an appointment. At first, we were skeptical "Are we getting ripped off here" But ultimately what won us over was the beautiful vison of keeping us warm any time without having drama. We can pay to fix problem once they happen, or we pay in advance to prevent them. Which one do you prefer?

What technology want us to become

To operate technology, we must operate like technology. If we are using technology for the things which we cannot do, we must do what technology does. Technology do not make us into computers when we operate them, we make ourselves into computers in order to operate them. Technology does not steal our spontaneity from us; we set our spontaneity aside ourselves. When we use technology to achieve whatever it is we desire, we cannot have what we desire until we have finished the technology which we use.

The ultimate goal of technology is therefore to eliminate itself, to become silent, to become omnipresent, invisible. We do not purchase a smartphone, for example. It's not technology we are buying at all, but what it makes us become. A perfect radio will draw no attention to itself, it will make it seem that we are in the very presence of the source anywhere and at any time. When most effective, the technology of communication allows us to bring the experience of others into our place, anywhere and at any time. The technology of collaboration allows us to work better together with the 'comfort of our home'. Technology is in a way contradictive.

I cannot use technology without using it with another. I do not talk to the phone; I talk with someone on the phone. I listen to someone on Spotify. In our construction industry we use technology to compute business transactions. To that degree that the way we work together in a project depends on such technology, the connecting medium makes each of us an extension of itself. If your business activities cannot translate into data recognizable by the software which I use, I can have no business with you. The effective technology that allows us to work better together is most effective when it's omnipresent, then we operate in such a way that we reach our desired outcome without operating like a computer.

Connected

My digital focused friend asked one time, "What does the word connect mean to you, and can you share this in a five-minute riff in our next team call? That was a great question! My riff went like this: The word Connect is part of Connected. Connected to other people with a shared interest across the world with a common language. Connected Connections are built on trust.   I have to give first my trust before I receive your trust. Trusted Connections will expand into culture. Culture is the people like us are doing the things like this. So, when learning and sharing are part of this culture, the people who are learning the most are the people who are sharing the most. From Connect to Connected, from centralized to decentralized, from not trusted to trusted connected people where we go from knowledge into thinking based on a growth mindset.

Gifts

Using Facebook is free, using LinkedIn us free, YouTube is free, even publishing a book on Amazon is free. We can go on and by finding examples but if you are not paying for something, you are not the customer, but you are the product. If someone is turning you into a product because it's helping them and not you. This is interesting because there is a disconnect between the old world and the new. But there have been other media and communication platforms that users didn't immediately pay for. This is how a lot of television and radio worked. How can you do that for free? LinkedIn or Google or Amazon is not just in the business of providing a service. It is also in the business of farming data, figuring out what people really want. From the old world to the new world, from disconnect to connect.

What do people want

What do people want? Let's start with our car, we don't want to buy car wash shampoo. We want to wash our car. The car wash shampoo is more a feature to wash our car. But that's not far enough, no one wants to wash their car. We want to have a clean car that will comes with washing the car. Actually, what we want is how we will feel once the car is clean.

But what does the word "want" means? The ego wants to want more than it wants to have. The shallow satisfaction of having is always replaced by more wanting. This is psychological need for more, that is to say, more things to own and to identify with. The ego is identifying with form, seeking our self, and thereby losing yourself in some of form. Forms are not just material objects like our car but representing thought forms which continuously arise in the field of our consciousness. It's like a mirror or if you want a twin of yourself.

The culture of high standards

Let's start first with a foundational question: "Are high standards teachable or not teachable?". If someone took you to a basketball team, they could teach you many new things, but they can't teach you to be taller. I would believe high standards are teachable. In fact, what I've seen is that people are good at learning high standards simply by exposure.

Bring a new person onto a high standards team, and they 'll quickly adapt. The opposite is also true, if low standards prevail, those too will quickly spread. If you have highs standards in one area, do you automatically have high standards elsewhere? High standards are more domain specific. Your team could have high standards on engineering or on inventing. But it could be that your team don't have high standards on customer care or on operational process. Understanding this point is important because it keeps you humble and it's critical to be open for improvements. What do you need to achieve high standards in a particular domain area? First, you have to be able to recognize what good looks like in that domain. Second, you must have realistic expectations for how hard it should be to achieve that scope or in other words, how much work it will take. Building a culture of high standards is well worth the effort, and there are many benefits. Culture is the people like us, are doing the things like this.

Naturally and most obviously, the people like us are going to build better products and services for the people who you seek to serve (this would be reason enough ?). And finally, high standards are fun! Once you 've tasted high standards, there's no going back

The focus effect

There are many ways to center a business. You can be competitor focused, you can be product focused, you can be technology focused, you can be customer focused, you can be engineering focused, you can be processed focused, you can be billable focused, you can be action focused, you can be result focused, and there are many more.

The focus is not the thing. It's always worth asking, do we own the focus or does the focus own us? In other words: do we own the customer which we serve, or does the customer own us? In the physical world, engineering companies will continue to use technology to reduce costs, but are they ready to transform the customer experience?

One thing about the people which we serve is that the expectations are never static, they go up, it's human nature. Yesterday's "wow" quickly becomes today's "ordinary." The cycle of improvement happening at faster rate than ever before. But how to stay ahead of the ever-rising customer expectations? There's no single way to do it, it's a combination of many things. But high standards (widely deployed and at all levels in your organization) are certainly a big part of it.

The tension of least resistance

What are the lessons that we teach a 2-year-old, 3-year-old, and a 4-year-old when we hand them an I-Pad? When we promise them something at Christmas? When they get dessert if they eat all their broccoli. The idea is that it's possible to grow up to be a citizen by being a consumer. That we send kids to school, not with two pairs of shoes but with closets filled with clothes. Clothes that change with the seasons because we don't want to get left out.

We couldn't go to the shopping mall during the during the pandemic and we missed it. And so, we shifted dramatically to browsing and spending time online. Not to browse and focus on things we can make better, but the focus on things we could buy with just one click. And sometimes one click is to many. So instead, we subscribe to something, it turns out that the company which sells Meal Kit Delivery like Hello Fresh is worth more than \$2.3 billion. By subscription because it's too much trouble to come up ourselves with new meals every day so the Meal Kit Delivery takes away the stress out of our mealtime.

And what about people who are following the manual and people who are writing the manual. What do we look for in someone who follows the manual? Follow instructions, seeks deniability, make good notes, does do what are asked but no more. Figure out to do just to do little less because otherwise the boss will ask to do a little bit more. Mostly, the one who is following the manual wonders if it's on the test. If people are keeping score, if they can stay where they are because it's so fraud to fall of the ladder because maybe they won't be a good consumer anymore. Where the giant industrialist seems to need more people who follow the manual or tolerate more people who follow the manual because they can have more consumers.

People who are writing the manual on the other hand are busy trying to solve interesting problems. Open new markets, innovate, discover new ways to connect with people, to enable cultural shifts to happen. Because all of those things, those initiatives we take, those efforts with sometimes the risk to change things. This is the work of people who are writing the manual. It's not always the profit what motivates, but it can be to get people better health by better food or to develop new technologies because all of those things use the skills of the people who are writing the manual.

So, it's probably not too late but we have to start the conversation and asking the questions: What will we do once we have enough people who are following the manual? And what about consumers, what will we do if enough people have enough stuff? What we know about the people who like to write the manual is that they desire their freedom. the freedom to innovate, the freedom to make decisions, the freedom to lead, and they are perhaps fewer good consumers, but they are making things better by making better things for people who care.

North star

If you hired a chef for your restaurant where your family members are waiting for dinner. If you have spent enough time ensuring you and your chef are aligned on exactly what types of foods will make the family happy, who eats what and why, the portions to make, and which type of foods should be cooked, rare, medium, or well. Your high-performing chef will be ready to select and cook the meals but without oversight.

However, if you hired a high-performing chef and give the free range to cook what he/she wants, but you haven't shared that your family hates salt and that any salad dressing with sugar will be rejected by all. It's likely your family wont' like the meal delivered to their plates. In this case, it's not your chef's fault. It's yours. You hired the right person, but you didn't provide enough context. You gave the chef freedom, but you and your chef were not aligned. Of course, in a company, it's not about one chef cooking for one family. Instead, there are many layers of leadership which makes creating alignment more complex but align, align your team on a north star so you can cook meals with oversight.

Success does not wait

If you are a football coach and playing the European football final and give the youngest players the responsibility to do the penalties, you risk losing the match. If you are running a hospital emergency room and give junior nurses the context to make decisions themselves with no oversight, people might die. If you are manufacturing airplanes and don't have plenty processes ensuring every part is assembled perfectly, the possibility of deathly accidents increases.

The question here is if your goal is error prevention or innovation? If your goal is innovation, making a mistake is not the primary risk. Although many retailers have gone out of business as increasing of people who shop online. That has changed the priority of coming up with fresh and new ways to get customers into the stores. Whether you're in the business of inventing toys for children, selling cupcakes, designing roads and bridges, or running a restaurant with fusion cuisine, innovation is one of the primary goals.

To encourage original thinking, don't tell your team what to do and make them check boxes.

Give them context to dream big, the inspiration to think differently and the space to make mistakes along the way.

What is the office for?

If we took office workers or executives from the nineteen sixties into the 2021 office. They will be shocked, shocked at the informality of information flow, shocked at the way people were dressed, the way they talk with each other, shocked that the office has dramatically shifted in sixty years.

We forgot to have a conversation about what the office is even for. Because the office might be for a lot different thing now. The first thought is that if a job is done repeatedly without a lot of innovation it is probably going to be outsourced. Because organizations are figuring out for example that they don't need to build themselves an email server, because they can pay an e-mail service twenty euro a month. They know what the spec is of what they need, and they can just outsource it to somebody else. If you call a company and you think you're talking to the customer service department, you might talk to a call center (interesting phrase, call center.)

A big argument for the physical proximity at the office is communication. If we are putting e-mail as one of the best ways to communicate from one person to another. Physical proximity is essential. But the rules changed, they changed with the telephone, they changed with e-mail and most of all they changed with Microsoft Teams. Because email, eliminates time. You don't have to be in the same moment to communicate with somebody.

Microsoft Teams eliminates space, you can communicate with somebody else even if they're not in the building. That it's worth noting that most large organizations have more than one office anyway and even more home offices. So, we had already drifted from the idea that you need to see someone face-to-face to communicate with them. But business travel, people travelling all over the world at a great carbon cost, kept growing and growing because there's something to be said for in-person communication

The transformation of the office

There's another kind of office. The kind of office that people talk about, by people who have the time to talk about change and this is the office whose job is not to figure out how not to screw up, its job is to change things. That's the reason companies pay a lot for this kind of work and it's hard to find people who will bring the energy and the passion to a problem and to come up with an original interesting solution who can actually grow market share not just maintain it. Who can solve interesting problems and there are offices now and then that add to that magic?

An office of a good, exciting movie like the front page where newspaper people are pushing each other for the scoop.

Where we are not talking about how we go to work, not simply to find out our place in a pecking order hierarchy, to play it safe to get through the day. When Amazon's Seattle Headquarters decided to build a different kind of office, they did all of those things because they wanted to transform a once-sleepy neighborhood of warehouses and shipyards into a buzzing technology hub. They were intent on changing things, changing things in a big way but like most organizations as they got bigger, they lost the thread so maybe they kept the fancy food but most of the people who work at a big organization are not trying to change anything.

They simply trying to keep things the way they are because they want the stock price to go up on a regular basis. So going forward, the question we need to ask is what kind of office we need. Is it about how to put on a show for the boss with the people who work for the boss or the people who work for the people who work for the boss? Is it a show about how many hours we put in so we would better be on that Teams call to show our compliance and our obedience

Because that show is really expensive and it's expensive if are you doing it from home and it's expensive when you are doing it in the office? A lot of these big organizations are going to take a look around and say we don't need that much compliance. We don't need that many people and there is going to be a move to hollow out a lot of the overhead in these institutions. Because technology, coordination, makes it much easier to get away with fewer people. Technology isn't going to wait around and organizations that need to go fast that need to innovate that need to connect people those organizations might not decide that the office of the future looks a lot like the office in the past. They might decide that what is in front of them is this massive opportunity to coordinate the activity of committed people who do emotional labor, soft skills, real skills, and insight to the table to put together resources and opportunities to make things better by making better things. There's no chance we're going back to the office of the nineteen sixties, and I think there's little chance we're going back to the 2018 office.

The jazz band

The Industrial Revolution was the transition to new manufacturing processes. During this industrial era there were pockets of the economy, such as advertising agencies, where creativity thinking drove success, and they managed on the edge of success. Such organizations accounted for just small percent of the economy. But now, with the growth in importance of intellectual property and creative services, the percentage of the economy that is dependent on nurturing inventions and innovation is much higher and continually increasing.

But there's a-but there is always a-but, isn't it? Most engineering companies are still following the paradigms of the industrial revolution that have dominated wealth creation for the last three hundred years. In today's information age we see also that in many companies and on many teams, the objective is no longer error prevention and replicability. On the contrary, it's creativity and speed. In the industrial era, the goal was to minimize variation and in the creative companies today, maximizing variation is more essential.

In this new situation, the biggest risk isn't making a mistake or losing consistency: it's failing to invent new products, to attract top talent, or change direction quickly when the rules of the game shifts. Consistency and repeatability are more likely to squash fresh thinking than to bring your company profit. A lot of little mistakes, while sometimes painful, help the organization learn quickly and are a critical part of the innovation cycle. In these instructions, rules and process are no longer the best answer. A symphony isn't what you're going for, build a jazz band instead. Jazz emphasizes individual spontaneity. The musicians know the overall structure of the song but have the freedom to improvise, riffing off one another other, creating incredible music. Of course, you can't just remove the rules and processes., tell your team to be a jazz band, and expect it to be so. Without the right conditions, chaos will ensure. Begin by to hear the music, building this culture because you can't ignore constant change. When it all comes together, the music is wonderful!

The games we play

Chess is a game like I to play, 64 squares, 32 pieces the rules can fit on two sheets of paper. The rules are the rules, you play the game, you can lose the game, or you can win the game and some people don't want to play chess. Because the game is a little trivial, it's trivial in the sense of it's not going to affect the outside world and it's something that a lot of people are not very good at playing chess. It doesn't make them feel good to play a game that they are not good at, and this create moments of tension because it's not so much fun as it should be. The game theory helps us understand that a game involves three things:

- Inputs
- Decisions
- Resources

There are multiple players and when the input changes, new decisions are required. Those decisions are actually decisions because there isn't an infinite number of resources, and you don't have unlimited time and unlimited power to do everything. So, you have to choose, and these choices have consequences, and it leads to outputs. Understanding the abstraction that we get, when we look at things in the world as a game. It's helping us understanding how the world works and how to make it better.   What do I talk about? LinkedIn is a game. It's pretty simple, maximum 3000 characters and 20 posts per 24 hours. These are the basic rules, and someone included the hashtag option. The game keeps getting refreshed all the time, new players show up. New input from the outside world shows up and people devote themselves to playing, not realizing that they are not customers of LinkedIn, but they are the product. That excitement, that disappointment that fear of sharing when you're using LinkedIn. That is a byproduct to get you to come back and use LinkedIn some more, so you can see more posts, LinkedIn is a game.   Now with this understanding we can all go to a new level of abstraction which is, some people showing up inventing games that are played on somebody else's board

The biggest game we play

If we look at the games that are pushed onto our culture which might benefit the game master but have significant side effects. So, what is the biggest game of all?

The biggest game is the meta game, and that meta game is the game of individuals seeking to make money by playing with open markets and capitalism. That game dynamic did not exist 800 years ago. But the dynamics of capitalism that people play who start winning and start playing harder that game turns out to be something that politicians have no choice but to play, and around and around it goes. If you want to change the culture, it really helps to play a game so that people who are trying to play the game of capitalism will go along with the change you seek to make. If you want to get rid away of carbon and save the planet.

One way to do it, is with cap and trade, so that people can make a profit, limiting carbon and one way you can do it, is by investing in technology that drives down the price of solar. Because we have seen in the last few years as solar has gotten cheaper nobody is building coal power plants and lots of people are building solar and wind power plants, some are doing it because they'd like their grandchildren to survive but many are doing it because it's a great strategy in the game and like chess, the basic fundamental rules behind capitalism are super simple.

Find something, someone wants to buy that you can sell for more than it cost you to make it and repeat. And then add it to the master of level game, which is to invest in people who are playing that game and so now it's becoming a higher level of abstraction.

Chapter Three – Transformation

Better questions lead to better answers which might lead to better outcomes. The last forty-five Saturdays I spent time studying and now it was time to see it from a bigger perspective. My digital focused friend asked me once to focus on what examples do we see in the industry. But have you ever asked yourself the following question?

"Why do we create still the same way the expected deliverables like we were doing ten years ago?"

Let's start from a bigger perspective. The industrial system we all live in is outcome based. We trust the system and the people we work for to give us what we need: certainty, status etc.

As long as we're willing to continue down the path, they've set out for us. The deal is simple: follow the recipe and you will get the outcome the system promised you.

But what happens when your world changes? Your world turns upside down, and the shifts around you can be extreme. Suddenly, you don't get what is guaranteed. And the tasks you are asked to do just aren't as engaging as you would like them to be.

The important work, the creative work, the work we really want to do. Doesn't come with a recipe. It follows a different pattern. Because when we do something for the first time, it's not as linear outcome-based recipe. That's where the might lead to better outcomes comes in.

The industrial system we all live in is outcome based. It's about guaranteed productivity in exchange for predicted labor. But if we choose to look for it, there is a different journey available to us. This path could be followed by the people like us who seek change, who hopefully want to make things better. It's a path defined by resilience and generosity, it's outward focused and not dependent on incentives or applause. It's about what excite us and share it with the people who we care about. Your creative work is about finding a pattern, find your way to serve the people you care about, share it and making magic, your magic.

If we don't follow the recipe but really asks our self how to make things better, it will create tension. But successful innovators don't ask their customers, client's, users to do something else. They ask them to become someone different. Facebook asks their users to become more open and sharing their personal information. Successful innovators ask users to embrace new values, new skills, new ideas, new expectations, new dreams. They transform their customers. Successful innovators make better innovations by making better clients and change them from one emotional state to another.

Like my digital focused friend suggested, it's about asking better questions; what do you want the people you seek to serve to become?

Transition

I started to see engineering products differently with all my Saturday study sessions. What does traditional mean and what does digital mean? When we look around, we see that we go from traditional retail to digital retail. From traditional newspaper to digital news and in our industry from traditional engineering to digital engineering. I learned from my friend that we should use technology within our teams or company where it has the most transformational impact.

Tradition is part of culture and culture is group habit, the culture is the people like us, do things like this, we must figure out who the people like us are because not everyone is people like us and not all things are things like this.

Transition to Product-as-a-Service

An outcome-based model drives a company to transform into customer-focused and thereby changes the innovation process. It's not a race to the bottom but a race to the top, it's transforming from acting downstream to upstream. The product-as-a-service business model leads to significant shifts both within and beyond the organization. Where we go from selling products to selling outcomes, and customers who are used to buying products also need to be educated and convinced about this shift. As we move forward to a demand-based economy, access and not ownership of products, will drive the success of the business in the engineering market. Digital Engineering, not traditional engineering, provides a new set of opportunities if companies are willing to rethink their business model so it can truly improve people's lives.

Is your company acting downstream or upstream? If you imagine a lightbulb, perhaps one from Philips. What kind of business do you think Philips Lighting is in? Perhaps you are thinking that Philips Lighting is selling lightbulbs, so perhaps Philips Lighting is a product-based business.

Let's go back in time, it's April 2015. Amsterdam's Schiphol Airport, Europe's fourth-busiest airport, reached an agreement with Philips and Cofely, the global leader in lighting, to pay for "lighting as a service" in its terminal buildings. Schiphol pays only for the light it uses, while Philips maintains ownership of all light bulbs and remains responsible for their maintenance and upgrade.

With this new business model Philips is no longer selling light bulbs (Downstream). Instead, it is being paid for the light used by its customer (Upstream). Because Philips had great interest to make sure that the light bulbs last longer or particular components can be replaced very easy and not replacing the entire light bulb. As a result, Philips developed special lighting bulbs that will last 75% longer than the conventional way and achieved 50% reduction in energy consumption.

The closer we look the less we see

When we look around, we see that digital technologies are reshaping the civil engineering and construction landscape. Product-based business models will be disrupted by service-based business models. New skills are needed in our world of product innovation and engineering transformation.

Where the challenge is and where the opportunity is to turn the traditional thinking leader in a forward-thinking leader. It looks like that the better we know what kind of success we want the more focused we are on the result we want to achieve. Focused on catching the ball, focusing on cost cutting, focusing on problem solving. Is it true that the closer we look the more details we see or is it the closer we look the less we, see?

The Dutch bicycle company Vanmoof received complaints that many of its bikes were damaged during shipping. It was getting expensive for the company and annoying for their clients. Vanmoof solution? They started printing images of flat-screen televisions on the shipping boxes, which are very similar in shape to the flat screen TV boxes. The results > 70-80% reduced damaged bicycles!

Playing the infinite game

Going Digital is an infinite game. It's not a game where finite players put play into time, the infinite players put time into play. Finite players are not trained only to anticipate on future possibility, but to control the future, to prevent it from altering the past. Infinite players continue their play is the expectation of being surprised. The infinite player does not expect only to be amused by surprise, but to be transformed by it. Finite games are played to be won. Whatever is not done in the interest of winning is not part of the game. The outcome of a finite game is the past waiting to happen. Whoever plays forward a certain outcome desires a particular past. The purpose of a finite game is to bring play to an end. With victory of one of the players, each finite game is played to end itself.

Infinite games cannot be ended, it cannot be repeated but it can become culture. Since the rules of play in an infinite game are freely agreed to and freely altered. Playing the infinite game creates culture which is both adopted and transformed by the infinite players.

Culture and cultural tradition is an infinite game. It's the people like us are doing the things like this. If the people like us are making things better by making better things with no boundaries. If that is the culture where you are in, then anyone can be participant in that infinite game and play it anywhere and at any time.

The transformation of your creation

Porsche Passport is a monthly subscription plan that offers members unlimited swaps between models at the touch of an app. Porsche cars are delivered and picked up by concierge anywhere a user chooses within their service area. No clients, but users. It's moving away from ownership and toward access. It's tilting away from the value of owning copies to the value of accessing networks.

The creation that has been valued by the networks will inevitable be transformed in some version - until something different. The more powerful the invention or creation the more likely and more important it is that it will be transformed by others.

Transformation is powerful because "transformation' is another term of becoming. "Transformation" acknowledges that the creations we make today will become and should become, something else tomorrow.

What does Porsche want their members to become? Porsche wants them to become increasingly more flexible, appreciate more the individual choice and feel more respected when they show up with their Porsche car. How do you transform your creation so that it will benefit the people who you care about?

A-B-C-D

A-B-C-D or 'always connecting the dots' is one of Sir Richard Branson's mantras. Steve Jobs said: "You can't connect the dots looking forward, you can only connect them looking backwards."

The point is to encourage people to question how the dots are connected. In most organizations, people join the dots the same way that everyone else does and always has done. This preserves a status quo. Because one day someone comes along and connects the dots in a different way, which lead to an entirely different understanding of the world. That's what happened with the people in the story telling workshops and the Premier Scholar Program which I recently delivered to a global audience. Where we started to change culture, connecting the dots by looking back and encourage to do it differently. Where I was amazed by the great stories and I realized that if you want something you never had, you have to do something you never did.

Difficult conversations

People spend weeks, months, years avoiding them. Difficult conversations get our society stuck, or the fear of the difficult conversations. We avoid talking about financial problems we have or the changes in our climate because we don't want to have a difficult conversation. What makes it a difficult conversation? Most people agree when our house is on fire, and everybody is asleep that it's not a difficult conversation to wake up everybody and get out of the house.

What makes it's difficult? We want to have two things and not one thing. If all we want is one thing and get out of the house, it's obvious what we want. It's difficult when we want two things, we want to change them, and we want to like it. We want someone to stop what they are doing, and we want them not to be mad about us. We want to change their behavior and we want them to stop doing what they are doing. We want to change their output and want them that they respect us. When we want to do two things, the whole conversation is going to be much more difficult to do.

Let's break this down: first, when we have the authority to lead the conversation and we don't care what the other cares about us it's not a difficult conversation. When you are waiting in line and the security officer corrects you because you are in the wrong line it's not a difficult conversation. Because the security officer feels confident and has the authority and is not experiencing this as a difficult conversation. But when one of those two things are not true it's going to be a difficult conversation. The easiest way to move forward we either can figure out how to gain authority or decide that we don't care because the house is not on fire and perhaps it's okay to be direct and simply not to have a difficult conversation without a lot of concern about the other side.

But most of the time we are stuck, we are stuck because we want them to change and to like it. It's important to get acceptance. Acceptance says: Where you want to go is where I want to go and the easiest way to move on with a difficult conversation is to spend much more time on acceptance.

The Angry Dog

If we encounter an angry dog, the question is not, do we want to adopt the angry dog in our home with two little kids? The question is, how would we engage with this angry dog so that it will not bite us. Empathy is what will get us there, because the angry dog is angry because what is done to it, the dog is angry because how it was raised, because the angry dog it's afraid or that it learned to be territorial. So, if we know what is going on in the mind of the angry dog, we will start learning how to treat the angry dog how it wants to be treated.

Because we are spending a lot of money on systems, on offices and other things, but we don't always spend that much on people. If we start educating people so that they understand, we should start by understanding who they are, what they are, and what make them tick. The point is, if we are just trying to get them change, they're not going to do it. People don't resist change; they resist being changed. We've got to make it appeal to people, to want to do better, to change, to be more productive.

If we want people in organizations to understand themselves, we've got to understand ourselves. If we are going to lead people, we've got to do what we want them to do, because there is no point in telling people to do something if we are not doing it ourselves.

Be careful who you owe

Capitalism is based on debt and here's the simple math: if you can buy a machine that let you be more productive, you will be able to gain market share and make a profit. That machine ends up being an asset of the company. That machine cost you money more than your competitors were willing to spent. To get that money you went into debt. You pay back this debt because over time you make enough of a profit that the machine pays for itself.

The very nature of capitalism has always been about building an asset, a property, maybe it's land, maybe it's machine and let you have more leverage and make more money. While we are in the fourth industrial revolution the question is:

- What are we going into debt for?
- And what kind of debt are we going into?

There is education debt, sleep debt, in the software world there is technical debt. There is also this idea of personal technical debt. Because in your life you've got a coffee machine and a dishwasher and a car and a laptop and a phone and all of them require you to be the head of maintenance. Figuring out what you want to keep up with which leads to what we really need to understand here is as knowledge workers, and that is the idea of project debt.

When a good project starts falling behind, management probably says: " Hire more people" and then we will get it done. As we add more people, there will be more management and more meetings and more communication and more bottlenecks and in fact when you added enough, the project will come perhaps even to a standstill. It doesn't actually go faster, it goes slower. Because project debt rises. Part of going forward in our project-based economy is figuring out smart ways to use the network to reduce the linear growth of project debt. Because if people are in Teams meeting all day long, nobody has time to get anything done.

Technical debt is not just the maintenance you need to keep your old systems running. It's in fact that you can't reach higher because your systems don't support it, so technical debt overlaps with project debt. When we take on projects, yes, they help us leverage what we want to do. But no, they don't always open the door for us to do the things after that but keeps us away from the next thing. The alternative is to realize is that we have to be much better to say no, because saying yes means inviting technical debt. And that technical debt, it needs to come with productivity that leads to possibility so we can invent the next thing which we call innovation. Be careful who you owe because who you owe decides who you become.

Chapter four – Becoming digital

I was at the point with an understanding what Digital meant. But what is the difference of doing digital and becoming digital? It's the key to success and I realized that generic work is replaceable. A generic can of beans can come from any company because they are all the same. But genre permits us to be original. It gives a framework to leverage. Drama movies are a genre, so is poetry a writing genre but why do you need genre for? Shawn Askinosie (https://askinosie.com/) has changed the way millions of people grow, sell, and eat fine chocolate. First, he began with a simple genre: "This is a chocolate bar." Then, he extended it to, " This is a handmade chocolate bar." It's worth noting that there's no mistaking what he makes. His packaging, customer relation, delivery systems – they all fit the genre.

Baldwin, Zev Siegl and Gordon Bowker (cofounders Starbucks) didn't invent coffee but changed the way people drink the types of coffee. Porsche passports didn't invent new cars but changed the way people use their cars by becoming more flexible. Daniel Ek and Martin Lorentzon (founders Spotify) didn't invent music, but the company changed the way how, where and when people are listening to their favorite music. Transformation begins with leverage and you build leverage by beginning choosing a genre. Not focusing on the crowd but by focusing on the smallest viable audience.

Inevitable

The movies, music, books, and games that we access, they live in clouds of computers. Working seamlessly together and act as one large computer. They are invisible but clouds run our digital lives. Where possession is not important as it was once. Accessing is more important than ever, where we go from products to services. From what is mine to what is from us.

My letter on my laptop. If we use the cloud, "my" letter appearance on my laptop where we can see the letter on my tablet or phone and work on it – edit, add, delete, modify as if it were "their" letter. Changes made on any of those copies will appear simultaneously – in real time- on all other copies anywhere in the world. Each instance of the letter is much more than just a copy. Each person experiences the distributed copy as the original on their device. Each of the dozen copies is authentic as the one on my laptop.

In the future, Artificial intelligence can automatically correct spelling. AI might also could do fact check statements in our letter or include hyperlinks.

Cloud computing and AI moves our work from individual ownership and migrate to the shared world of the people like us are doing the things like this.

Doing digital and becoming digital

Transform an existing team or organization is a challenge, especially given the immense power of digital technologies. There is a difference between "doing" digital and "becoming" digital. Transformation is powerful because "transformation" is another term of becoming. "Transformation" acknowledges that the creations we make today will become and should become, something else tomorrow.

The people who are affected by the change of digital transformation need to know how they are going to be taken care of. The following type of questions need to be answered:

- What are we changing to?
- What is the role we need to play?
- How will we they be rewarded, what is in for me?
- What is the transformation and why is it critical for us?

This goal of "becoming" digital is key to achieving digital transformation. The organization can "do" digital as part of a one-time transformation, but to achieve ongoing market leadership for your team or company it needs to "become" digital. The difference between "doing" digital and "becoming digital" is being involved and being committed, which is like ham and eggs – the chicken was involved, but the pig was committed.

The changemakers

If you own a company or leading a team and the work is all about buying you hours, then the smart employee should sell those hours to the highest bidder. But if work is the place where we spend halve our lives, if work is about meaning, if work is about connection and growth then we should start building a great culture where that sort of thing is valued and expected.

The innovative organization has an open, healthy culture at all levels that shape and reshape strategy. Because culture beats strategy – culture is strategy.

Well then, the word will spread, the people who have a choice they will choose your organization. If skill is what you have, if skill is what you sell, if skill is what you are able to grow and create. Well, the marketplace will pay you for that thing that you are building. Because, if you are doing a job that can be done by a computer, the computers are going to do that job.

For us to thrive as organization in the future we have to become the sort of organization that employees of the future want to work for, and those customers of the future want to buy from. Not because we are in the race to the bottom but because we are in the race to the top!

Lost in obsession with outcome

We live in an outcome based-focused culture and perhaps we don't always recognize it. The car washer guy doesn't get credit for effort: he gets credit if the car shines. A short-term focus on outcomes means that we decide if a book is good by its bestseller rank, if a singer is good based on winning a TV talent show. If children in school doing good based on whether or not they passed the test with great results and perhaps won a trophy.

Lost in obsession with outcome is the truth that outcomes are the results of the quality of the action. Good actions repeated over time lead to better outcomes.

Another way to look at it is focusing on outcome based is focusing on what is missing. The book on Amazon rank 2938, the singer did not win the TV talent show. The children didn't pass the test (and perhaps we tell ourselves that we are not good parents.)

We allow others to live in our head, reminding what is missing in our life. Our practice begins with imperative that we embrace a different pattern, a pattern that offers not guaranteed outcome. If we think hard, not focusing on what is missing, work hard, your digital engineering work find an audience for whom it's meaningful. It might not be what we want to hear, but it's true.

The network effect of interoperability and open source

What is more likely to lead to more innovation? Centralized control, who is allowed to plugin into the system. Or an open system, where someone who has a great idea and can plug into it. What does established players wants to do, control contribution, control technology, control labor, control access to users, control government regulations to keep innovators from coming along in a closed system. This battle is never ending.

What do consumers or users want? One of the abilities for innovators might be to plugin into existing systems, in other words: Creating a system where independent people are able to market where interoperability and open comes into play.

Interoperability is the act of making a new product or service work with an existing product or service. The technical ability to plug one product or service into another product or service. When you buy a pair of headphones you knew that the device which you are go to plugin will work.

Open Source is freely accessible source code and interoperable is how things interact. We agreed on standards, protocols and specifications that assure all these systems do interoperate. If we use Open Source for our standards to increase interoperability it doesn't mean they are interchangeable, they are still the standards, but it might create a network effect. The people like us are using and sharing information like this. The network effect builds a chain of interoperability, all of the organizations, all of the inventors, all the people who build the chain of me and you, don't know each other. Not that they don't know each other but they never communicated because it's not necessary to communicate because there is a network of interoperability.

It could be that you are participating in one of the interoperability trends in the infrastructure market. Perhaps you are not aware, but you are part of changing culture. The people like us in the Netherlands are going to use BIM basis Infra, the people like us in Finland are using Inframodel schema, the people like us in Norway are using Sosi format. This Digital Engineering journey of the people like us who are interested to make interoperability better are following the five steps of Digital Engineering by the changing the culture.

What the robots can't do

Personal trainers or regular gym, premium class or economy class, glamping, or camping? What do they have in common? It's the increase of cost but more importantly it's the level of attention which means the increased level of human experience.

We give our complete attention to the creators of these experiences. Our attention is worth a lot. Not coincidentally, humans excel at creating and consuming experiences. This is no place for robots. If you want a glimpse of what humans do when the robots take our current job, look at the experiences.

That's where we will spend our money and that's where we will make our money. We will use technology to produce the ordinary things and will make experiences in order to avoid becoming ordinary our self.

It's not a race to the bottom, don't follow the crowd. Instead find an edge and make things better by making the people who you serve more valuable to you. It's about the experience, what do you want the people who you seek to serve to experience?

The engine of question makers

Our society is moving from tangible products to intangible products, from belongings to access, from finite games to infinite play. It's moving from the certainties of answers to the uncertainty of questions. Ironically, the best questions are not always questions that lead to better answers. What makes a good question?

- A good question challenging existing answers.
- A good question is not concerned with a correct answer.
- A good question cannot be predicted.
- A good question will be the sign of an educated mind.
- A good question is what humans are for.

The technologies of generating answers will continue to be essential, so much that answers will become omnipresent, instant, reliable. The technologies that help generate good questions will be valued more.

Question makers will be seen as the new engines in our construction market and generate new possibilities. Better questioning is simply more powerful than answering. The engine you use to ask better questions creates better answers, which leads to better decisions.

What kind of question maker engine do you think will lead to better questions during design or construction?

The recommendation engines

Who doesn't like – or need – good advice? The "good" in "good advice" is firmly in the mind of the engineers like us. It's the right recommendation at the right time what matters.

Bluntly, technology is taking over advice. Sooner rather later, most people in most places won't make decisions about what to do or where to go without the help of a recommendation engine. They want their recommenders giving them greater confidence and clarity about making the right choice.

The recommendation-as-innovation infiltrates and influences the questions people ask, where we go from "How can people create more valuable innovations?" to "How can innovation create more valuable people".

The emphasis shift from innovation as output to innovation as investment for input of capabilities. The recommendation engines have become not just core technologies but essential organizing principles for our experience.

What kind of recommendation engine can you think off in our construction market?

Mind and machine the recommendation experiences

We like – or need – good advice. The "good" in "good advice" is firmly in the mind of the engineers like us and the clients which we serve. It's the right recommendation at the right time what matters, in fact everything is a recommendation. How are your clients experiencing your recommendation, are they curious? Energized? Motivated? Appreciated? Bored? When everything is a recommendation then the recommendation experience is everything.

This is also true for movies, music, shopping, travel, dining, and socializing. It's not local but global. People from Amsterdam to Istanbul to Singapore to Sydney to New York expect good recommendations. The experience is tightly connected with the expectations, people don't just demand better recommendations; they want a better recommendation experience. It's the difference between good cooking and fine dining. It's about the ambiance, the service and all enhance both the food and the experience.

The recommendation engines draw upon multidisciplinary knowledge and expertise to deliver greater value and inspire greater client confidence. They seek to inform, advise, anticipate, share, build trust, delight, create community, personalize, self-learn and serve the needs of the engineering company and the client. Increasing awareness is the first step where transparency and trust-building are central to how the recommendation aligns the client experience and client expectations. The recommender experience is essentially a story – a narrative about the good advice, which story can you think off which would resonate with the people who you seek to serve. The closer we look at something there is less to see the next time. Because we have seen most of it before, the same problems over and over again. But instead of focusing on catching the ball let's change our focus to the action of throwing the ball so we see more if we look closer.

Perfect Going Digital Journey

Perfectionism does not mean quality. Perfectionism is a way of hiding. Perfectionism is polishing something where people don't care about the polish. If you are going to launch a new airplane, it is not perfectionism to make sure it will never crash, that is simply one of the designs specs. Perfectionism is trying to consider every single possible objection and answering it. Perfectionism of our Digital Engineering journey means: making the list ever longer, delaying the project, adding to the budget, and not finding out what the people you seek to serve are actually ready for. Because we are going to believe that we will never get a second chance to make a first impression. We believe that what we ship isn't perfect and we will be shamed forever for when it comes time to change the world whatever we ship will not be perfect. It's a given; we cannot know if it's perfect because we haven't engaged with the people who we seek to serve. So, what we can do is figure out what's important and get what's important correct and then ship and learn and adjust. That when we do our digital transformation with resilience. What we have, is the chance to show up with the people we are seeking to change, the people we are seeking to serve and say: "Here I made this" and then watch what happened and then evolve it.

We're going to have a portfolio, if we're going to be resilient if we're putting down or bet in, in multiple areas, then we cannot do giant projects. Because we can't go all in on one and also have the resilience to be flexible with a few. So, the purpose of the screen is to highlight the fact that we have been following ourselves into thinking that we have to be perfectionists and that we have to do something that will truly change the world that we can brag about.

Instead, if we are resilient, if we are standing for something, for some group of people but that group might be smaller than our peers are hoping for. We have an advantage.

The advantage is that group, that smallest viable audience is a group we can earn trust with. That group, if we earn their trust if we delight them, they will tell the others and so it begins to spread, drip by drip.

Ultimate recommendation engines

Self-knowledge. Self-interest. Self-improvement. Self-Control. Self-Discovery. The idea and ideal of a "best self." Recommendation engines increasingly shape who people are, what they desire, and who they want to become. Consider, as a thought experiment, a recommender based on motivational speaker Jim Rohn's argues that "we are the average of the five people we spend most time with." Whether or not you agree, take that "who we are" heuristic and seriously. Similar videos which we see, the music we hear, places we eat, photos we share, games we play, things we buy and skills we learn. These are, after all people we spend a lot of time with.

Then realization hits: You want to be the average of the five best people you know. That's a thoughtful and intentional bet on self-discovery and self-improvement.

But wait! Why limit yourself to people you know? Why not draw inspiration, motivation, and insight from accomplished people you don't know? Perhaps you want to be average of your five favorite celebrities? The recommendations are tailored to your skills, time, and equipment. Do you want to be still the average of the five people we spend most time with? Maybe you want to be the average of the five greatest 3D designers in the world, or maybe you want to be the average of the five scripting gurus to improve design automation in your company?

The win of the twin

For the people who like music there is Spotify, for people who like movies there is Netflix. Interesting is that Spotify and Netflix are modeling the behavior of every single user, the taste is primarily based on listening or watching habits, what features the people use and in Spotify what artist they follow.

For the people who use Spotify, their listening habits are combined in the Discover Weekly playlist. This playlist is like a secret music Twin which Spotify put together. The music twin created by the Spotify recommendation engine empowers to make better choices than they might likely if you make them on your own.

If a music twin is already created of yourself by using Spotify, then we can also create a twin for the engineer, Engineering Twin, a twin for the client, Client Twin. There are three key organizing principles underlie the recommender Digital Twin technology.

Digital Twin as "Prediction" technology

Recommendation is everywhere and always about the future. What should stakeholders focus on, what is next? Those next are bundles of choices and options, it's about being resilient.

Digital Twin as a "Discovery process" technology

Predicting and discover what stakeholders will focus on.

Digital Twin as a "Production methodology"

Insights gleaned and gained to make the best decisions based on the best recommendation to produce deliverables.

The future of self is the future of recommendation. Recommendation will become fire and fuel for human capital transformation

Glimpse of the digital engineering future

Digital technology is leading the fourth industrial revolution, which allows the convergence of the digital and physical products. Where we go from centralized to decentralized production, where a machine no longer simply processes a product but where the product communicates with technology to tell exactly what to do. A great example is Siemens Smart Factory in Bavaria. It shows the future of construction industry 4.0 where a product controls their own manufacturing processes. In other words, their product codes tell the production machines what requirements they have, and which production steps must be taken next. In this vision of the fourth industrial revolution, the physical and virtual worlds will merge. The products will communicate with the production system in order to optimize the build process. Products and technology will determine among themselves which parts should be build first in order to meet the deadlines. Siemens's digital factory provides a glimpse of the future of manufacturing, which is the start in the new era of improved productivity in a wide variety of industries like Civil Engineering and the Construction market.

Feedback Loop

Last year, the people in our village where our kids go to elementary school were struggling. Accidents involving cars and kids were alarmingly frequent on the streets around the school. The municipality put up speed limits signs in order to get drivers to slow down, and police doled out tickets to violations. Engineers tried another approach, putting up dynamic speed displays. In other words, "driver feedback." Passing drivers got real-time data on their speed and a reminder of how fast they should go.

Experts were doubtful that this would help. Everyone has a speedometer on their dashboard. Furthermore, law enforcement doctrine has long held that people obey rules only when they face clear consequences for breaking them, why would the display influence driver behavior?

But they did. The drivers slowed down 14 percent; the average speed fell below the posted speed limit. But here is the thing: the dynamic speed display is a feedback loop and is about improving performance.

Digital integrated design in our road design projects can be seen as dynamic speed displays. We learn faster and accomplish more when we make giving and receiving feedback a continues part of how we collaborate and communicate in our projects.

Creating a feedback loop is a lot more difficult than putting up traffic signs but we should start implementing the feedback loop by the use of a common data model and common data environment. Where we start building a culture of feedback loops where each engineering discipline will have the opportunity to improve their performance and grow, grow together.

Screening

An idea is important, a fact is interesting, and a book or paper is an attention unit. But only a story, a good argument, a well-crafted narrative is amazing. Those stories will play across screens, everywhere we look, we see screens. The new digital creation tools have empowered a new generation of filmmakers, we headed toward screen ubiquity.

The screen demands more than our eyes. The most physically active we get while reading a book is to flip the pages. But screens engage our bodies. Touch screens respond to our fingers. Sensors in game consoles track our hands and arms and the newest screens track our whole-body movements. Screens trigger interaction and smart software can now read our emotions as we read the screen and can alter what we see next in response to our emotions.

Books or paper were good at developing a contemplative mind. Screens encourage more effective and interactive thinking. Books or paper strengthened our analytical skills. Screening encourages rapid patterns makings, associating one idea with another. Screening nurtures thinking in real time. We review together a design model and assign design tasks in real time while we see it. We come up and submit new ideas to make digital products better. Screens are instruments of the now.

But more important, our screens will also watch us. They are our mirrors and not to see our faces, but our selves. The screen becomes part of our identity and screens will be the first place we'll look for answers, news, for meaning and making decisions

Surrounded by stories

We're surrounded around by stories. Look around, wherever you are, surrounded by stories that have created value. You don't need a story about rice or potatoes you need to eat them. You don't need a story about a roof over your head, you need one to survive.

Once our basic needs have been taking care of all we've got left is the value we assign to stories. If a story is working, then we keep using it. The people who are trading cryptocurrencies are basically sharing a story about how things are going up in value. A story about potential. When it's analyzed like all stories al lot of it is not true. But when enough people believe the story, the story persist.

But there is moment that these stories intersect with real life. When a senior citizen who needs money to survive doesn't want their retirement funds to be worth zero. Where we see that big traditional companies, which were based on product base business models are getting in trouble and being disrupted by service-based business models.

Sooner or later stories will collide with the lives we live. But along the way it doesn't matter if a speedbump hits the story, if the story is strong enough and widely held enough, it will persist. We have to be really thoughtful which story we tell ourselves and why.

More valuable to us

People don't just adopt innovations. They alter them, adept to them and are changed by them. Pick any product, service or idea who matters. Facebook, Google, Boing, Walt Disney.

Successful innovators don't ask their customers, client's, users to do something else, they ask them to become someone different. Facebook asks their users to become more open and sharing their personal information. Successful innovators ask users to embrace new values, new skills, new ideas, new expectations, new dreams. They transform their customers. Successful innovators make better innovations by making better clients and change them from one emotional state to another. Googles gets smarter every time when someone makes a search and immediately acts on that information and improves the experience for everyone. Google continuously improves the capabilities of its searchers and vice versa. As the Google users gets smarter and more sophisticated, so does Google. Win / win. Just as Elon Musk automobiles created a new nation of drivers, Google's search engine(s) networked a new world of searchers. What does Google asked their users to become? People who don't think twice about spending a few moments to type in some words on their computer. Don't worry about the typos and quickly scan the list of available links. The user can be confident that the first few listed results would give the right results. Google did turn impatient people into people who appreciate the results at zero cost.

The easiest way to understand this new way of thinking is by answering yourself the question. What innovations did you say yes to over the last few years? Look hard at the product, service, or idea you have chosen. Whether physical, digital, medical, or social, those innovations helped who you are today. You picked them because how they transformed you from one emotion to another. Second, how have this changed you who you are? Start thinking seriously about how the embraced innovations have transformed you.

Let's take a tangible product which we all use. Look at your smartphone, how long have you used it? What are the five features, functions you have used most often? What is single most important impact your smartphone had on your life? How does that change you? The more innovatively you get value from your smartphone, the more impact it has on your life because it's addressing your emotional needs.

Once you accept the tangible reality that innovation changes in who you become, you begin to see what ability is acquired to empathize with your clients.

Find the people like us

When you believe in your idea so much that you ignore evidence that the people who you seek to serve don't like it. Or worse, they are totally disinterested because people don't need your product, they might want it, but they don't need it. People might decide to use your product, most of them they don't want it because it's your idea. They want it because of how it will make them feel. That's what they are buying: a feeling. Want we should be doing is to identify the feeling and start to connect, figure out the fears, dreams and help them to become the person they've dreamed of becoming.

Building a tribe takes all of the work we've already begun. Empathy, because we have to understand what people want from being in this tribe—we have to understand their worldviews, dreams, desires, and fears. Humility, because the tribe is not about you—it's about something far larger than you. Trust, because members of a tribe feel that they have each other's back. Tension, because tribes are defined as having insiders, which means there are also outsiders.

So, building a tribe takes work. Emotional labor not mechanized managing or coordinating. It takes leadership. It takes time (remember, trust and attention are earned with the consistent delivery of promises).   Maybe you could invent the tribe of long-distance non-Olympic runners, the way Nike did. Not likely. Far more likely is that you'll tap into existing tribal influences, the way Apple, Fox News, and thousands of other brands large and small have. "People like us do things like this."

Digital Twin- For us or to us?

If you buy a piece of software that runs in Windows, it's probably not easily run on your Mac and vice versa. The operating system is a series of rules, approaches the ways that software can work and if you're going to create an operating system you have a lot of responsibility.

Cities are one of the oldest operating systems in the history of humanity. A city is a series of rules. You can put a house in a city, you could open a store in a city you might have a park in the city. But all of these things whether the absence of them are defined by the operating system of the city itself. When we have an operating system of a city. We begin by making choices. In the early days, cities were defined by their need for water. If you don't have fresh water, humans can't survive. Part of the operating system of having that many people together, interacting with each other is not just law and order, because it's also public works

If we go back to computer operating systems. We don't have really a choice and that's the difference between software and the operating system. If you don't like a piece of software buy another one, as long as it doesn't have lock in. You have choices, you've committed to an operating system until someone change it like Apple or Microsoft, breaking it for millions of people who will start screaming and yelling.

But all of these are decisions, as profound as how to get the water into the city, decisions as profound as whether or not working for cars or trains.

Systems don't last forever because they're impacted by other systems and one after another pushing it forward. So here we are in this moment of time. Right on the precipice between open resilient systems and closed ones. Take a hard look at the new operating systems like Digital Twins because it's not always a Tim Cook that launches a new Operating System at some fancy conference. It could very well be that the operating systems of our future are already around us, and we are not seeing them or defining them if we are not pushing them to be better. Then they are not going to be for us or by us. They are going to be done to us until we have no choice but to live with them

The value of free

Free is hard to ignore. The top ten music videos have been watched (for free) over 20 billion times. It's not only music that is being copied freely. It's text, images, websites, designs, 3D models. Anything that can be copied will be copied for free. In this new digital world of infinite free digital duplication, copies are cheap – free, the only things truly valuable are those that cannot be copied. The technology is telling us that copies don't count anymore. In other words, when copies are superabundant, they become worthless. Things which can't be copied become scarce and valuable. When copies are free, focus on things which cannot be copied. Well, what can't be copied?

Trust cannot be copied and be reproduced in bulk. You can't download trust and store it in a database. You can't simply duplicate someone's else's trust. Trust must be earned; it cannot be faked. Since we prefer to deal with someone we can trust, we will often pay premium for that privilege. There are similar qualities or emotions to trust that are difficult to copy and thus become valuable in this digital world. The best way to see them is to start with asking better questions:

- Why would someone ever pay for something they could get for free?
- When they pay for something, they could get for free, what are they purchasing?

The uncopyable values are things that are "better than free" Free is good, but these are better since you'll pay for them.

Goals and machines

Can machines exhibit goal-oriented behavior? This question is not about consciousness or feelings, then the answer is obvious. "Of course, they can.". Since we can design them that way. We design dishwashers with the goal of cleaning the dishes, and clocks with the goal of keeping the time, heating in our houses with the goal to keep us warm.

If you look around and see what we build exhibits goal-oriented design, not goal-oriented behavior. A highway or bridge doesn't behave , it's merely sitting there and was designed to accomplish a goal.

The new goal-oriented behavior has the potential to be much more diverse, designed entities can have virtually any ultimate goal, even opposite ones. Stoves try to heat food and refrigerators try to cool food. Generators try to convert motion into electricity while motors try to convert electricity into motion. Gradually we learned to build machines with more complex goals, such as robotic lawn mowers or robotic vacuum cleaners.

When we build a machine to help us, it can be hard to perfectly align its goals with ours. A mousetrap may mistake your bare toes for a hungry mouse, with painful results. The mousetrap is happy to trigger because it has no clue what a person is. Many of such goals can therefore be solved by making our machines smarter and the more intelligent and powerful machines get, the more important it becomes that their goals are aligned with ours

Goal oriented design

Goal-oriented behavior of smarter machines and aligning with our goals isn't just important but it's also hard. Let's explore and what does "our goals" mean. First, we will split the big goals into sub goals:

- Making smarter machines learn our goals
- Making smarter machines adopt our goals
- Making smarter machines retain our goals

To learn our goals, smarter machines must figure out not what we do, but why we do it. If you ask a future self-driving car to take you to the airport fast as possible. And it takes you literally, you will get there chased by the police. There are many more examples which we can come up with and they are showing that we have to figure out what people really want. We need a detailed model of the people which we seek to serve. Once we have this model, we can figure out what people want even if they don't tell us, but by simply observing our goals-oriented behavior and learn also what our goals are.

DJ-Running

Interesting example is a research project DJ-Running. This is an emotion-based system for recommending Spotify songs to runners. People who are practicing running as a sport and want to be better and perhaps their goal is to the best. Most of the people who are running are listening to music during the development of this physical activity using their portable music players, mainly, mobile phones. Running with music can help to increase the runner's motivation, making hard training sessions much more pleasant as well as make the runner feel less alone but achieve in the meantime their goal. It learns runners emotional and physiological activity during the training sessions, to automatically recognize their feelings and to select, in real-time, the most suitable music to improve their motivation and performance.

Aligning our goals with smarter machines takes time. Learning, adopting, and retaining our goals is critical. Where technology is the omnipresent and here to serve us so we can be more creative. Because if smarter machines can do our job, they will do our job.

Take action

When you opened this book, you probably said," We have fantastic existing products and I have a fantastic idea, service or product to bring to the world and I need more people to going to use it. I have a problem."

That's why my digital focused friend once said that the Japanese value the power of the mirror the most, for it is only when we look into it that we find the truth. Fear is the main reason that people say." Play it safe." That goes for everything, careers, money, relationships. I spent many times after work sitting at a table with my friend, because here was a man who had not gone with the crowd. He was a man who did his own thinking. He also hate the word. "Can't" By now, I hope that you see infinite game of digital. Once you adopt a posture of service, of engaging with the culture to make change, the shift happens. Instead of asking, "How can I create more engineering products and let more people to listen to me". Ask now "How can I get the word out, how can I get more people let use my digital engineering product." I wish you great digital engineering journey and a fabulous gift called life!

Acknowledgments

The year 2021 is behind us but Ernst did commit himself for one year to study every Saturday for fifty-two weeks. Yes, there are fifty-two Saturdays which resulted in fifty-two subjects related to Digital Engineering. Digital Twin Consultant, Ernst van Baar takes you on an amazing journey but along the way there is a fork in the road. Which direction to go, the traditional engineering or digital engineering? The operating systems of our future are already around us, and if we are not seeing them or defining them if we are not pushing them to be better. Then they are not going to be for us or by us. They are going to be done to us until we have no choice but to live with them. And if you want to learn more how to build a culture I'm recommending you the book Digital Engineering, How to make better thins working better for you. During these Saturdays, if I can borrow great ideas and recombine them in interesting ways for the people who have great ideas and want to make digital engineering better, perhaps I can contribute something. In this book I borrowed from so many people and but in general I want to thank all the great work and where they turned me from outsider to insider, Always and endless love, thanks to Matthea, Lars, Niels van Baar!

Index

A

A-B-C-D, - 38 -

B

Be careful who you owe, - 41 -, - 43 -
Becoming digital, ii

C

classroom style., - 4 -
Connected, - 15 -
ii

D

Decisions, - 28 -
Difficult conversations, - 39 -
Digital Twin as, - 58 -
Digital Twin- For us or to us?, - 65 -
DJ-Running, - 70 -

F

Feedback Loop, - 59 -

G

Gifts, - 16 -

H

Happy- 11 -

I

Ideas, - 72 -
Inputs, - 28 -

J

Journey,- 10 -

M

Moving,- 13 -

N

North star, - 21 -

O

One friend, - 2 -

P

Perfect, - 54 -
8 -

R

Race, - 12 -
Service, - 11 -

T

Take action, - 71 -

Transition, - 33 -
Transition to Product-as-a-Service, - 33 -

U

Ultimate, - 56 -

About the author

Digital Twin Consultant, Ernst van Baar gives you the keys to implement successful Digital Engineering ideas, services, and products in your organization. In 2020 he published his first book: Digital Engineering – How to make better things working better for you. It's time to grow your new Digital Engineering engine. Because you want to disrupt before you are disrupted – make a change happen in our Digital Engineering world, not the next boring Digital Engineering product. If you want to be reach out, please feel free to send an e-mail to: baar@ernstvanbaar.com

Notes

Notes